WITHDRAWN
HARVARD LIBRARY
WITHDRAWN

Freud and Saint Paul

(*An exploratory study of two great men who have had a profound influence upon Western civilization*)

by
Carl T. Healer

DORRANCE & COMPANY
Philadelphia

Copyright © 1972 by Carl T. Healer
All Rights Reserved
ISBN 0-8059-1672-5
Library of Congress Catalog Card Number: 70-187015
Printed in the United States of America

The opinions or assertions contained herein are those of the writer and are not to be construed as official or reflecting the views of the Navy Department or the Naval Services at large.

To
Joe and Ann, Frank
and Walt

CONTENTS

	Page
Preface	vii
Acknowledgments	xi

Lecture

I	Pastoral Counseling — Introduction and Overview	1
II	A Theory of Personality — Freud	12
III	A Theology of Persons — St. Paul	20
IV	"Out, Damned Spot! Out!" A Study in Guilt	31
V	"Stripped, Naked I Stand" A Study in Shame	42
Bibliography		53

PREFACE

Since being introduced to Freud and psychoanalysis, I have maintained three major interests: one, an interest in psychoanalytic theory as a metaphysical system; two, an interest in psychoanalysis as a therapeutic process; and three, the possible relationship of Freud's basic concepts with what will be referred to as a "Theology of Persons."

The Psychoanalytic Theory of Personality is a beautiful and magnificent concept. Its literature seems inexhaustible. Efforts toward refinement are endless. I speak of this as a student enthralled with a great idea: as a student who struggles or aspires to understand a teacher he greatly admires, and as a student who, out of a deep interest in life experiences, has tried to form a synthesis of two great concepts: Freud's Theory of Personality and St. Paul's Theology of Persons.

Freud parlayed a break out. The symbolism seems important. The world was ready for a break out and a break away from a theological system that had held it in a dogmatic determinism. With its moralistic terrorism and its oppressive educational process, this system served only to drive man's worst proclivities underground.

Once Freud's idea freed itself from the prejudices of the milieu in which it was conceived and born, and broke the barriers of resistance to its popularization, it became revolutionary. Society had to take a new look at itself. Art, literature, religion, politics, education and the world of entertainment felt the impact of this new teaching. For many, it was the answer to a "creed outworn." For others, it was heresy. For still others, it was a fresh breeze blowing through the sails of an old ship in great need of refurbishing. Some saw in it a rare chance to revisit the old teachings by which they had lived. Some, caught in the "logjam" of a new concept and unable to work their way out, embraced the "new religion." Others tried to fuse the new psychology with their beloved theological views, but the marriage has not been too successful. Still others were able to work their way through to a more meaningful faith and a greater concept of theology—at least in its practical expression. Uppermost were the thoughts: if there was conflict, resolve and/or reject; if there was complement, refine and revitalize; and, in a pragmatic sense, if it worked, use it.

It has taken the writer a long time to reach the conclusions here presented, yet, they are by no means decisive. They are merely exploratory. Beyond that, nothing is offered but the hope that further study is encouraged. The ideas put forth are crystallizations of an inquiry which started as a research paper entitled "On the Origin and Nature of Guilt in Psychoanalytic Thought" during postgraduate studies in 1956. Having completed that project as a course paper and subsequent lecture to the group, I left the classroom with the feeling that I had not accomplished my task. While guilt appeared to be an important dynamic, there seemed to be something lacking, deeper and more personal. In short, while I was successful in my study, I was not content with my accomplishment.

Theologically, it seemed that too much emphasis was being placed on guilt (not that this is to be downgraded). People were not responding to the evangelical plea for open commitment and openness in daily living. Then one Sunday a very distraught woman said to me, "I wanted to make a commitment this morning, but my pride would not permit me. I was afraid of what people would think and say." I identified with her feeling for I too had experienced that same feeling many times.

So my quest continued. I knew the shame complex was the problem and that once I understood its nature and workings, I might be able to effect some change—certainly relieve some of the tension I personally felt at times. But I did not know or understand how it worked. Neither did I understand how it could unite with guilt to produce two very strong fears: the fear of punishment (in the sense of physical hurt) and the fear of rejection (in the sense of banishment). I knew most of us worked on the assumption that we could take our punishment as long as it did not mean rejection (or, to use a more emotionally charged theological concept, excommunication). The lectures will tell the rest of the story.

These lectures were written with the mental image of a classroom setting and were designed to be given to seminarians in particular. Having taught at the college level, the classroom is my home; yet, these discourses have not been formally given to that group. They have, however, been given to various groups across America, in Japan, in Hong Kong and on the high seas. Lecture no. I was given to the Neuro-Psychiatric Nurses School, National Naval Medical Center, Bethesda, Maryland, to the Chapel Guild of the Marine Corps Development and Educational Center, Quantico, Virginia and to the Journal Club of the Neuro-Psychiatric Service, U. S. Naval Hospital, Oakland, California.

In addition all the lectures were given to the Thursday Fellowship at the Marine Corps Base, Quantico, Virginia. This was a group of professionals and laymen composed of the post-psychiatrist, psychologists, doctors, clergymen and certain selected laymen who counselled people in a quasi-professional capacity.

ACKNOWLEDGMENTS

I am particularly indebted to Dr. Joseph Ross, Psychiatrist, and to Frank Connolly and Walt Collins, both Clinical Psychologists, for listening to the lectures, and for their frankness in discussing the form and content, and their encouragement. Dr. Ross, Mr. Connolly and myself, representative of the three major faiths (Jewish, Catholic, and Protestant), initiated the Thursday Fellowship.

I owe special thanks to Dr. William Sheppe, Jr., Associate Professor of Psychiatry of the Medical Center, University of Virginia for taking the time from his busy schedule to read and comment on the manuscript. Thanks is also due Dr. Bruce Rhodes, Neuro-Psychiatric Service, U. S. Naval Hospital, Yokosuka, Japan, who also took the time to read, to critique and discuss the manuscript. And to Monsignor John O'Conner, Captain, Chaplain Corps, U. S. Navy, a word of special thanks is extended for his encouragement to develop further the notion of a "Theology of Persons."

My sincere appreciation to Miss Sachiko Ogawa of Otsu, Japan for typing the original manuscript.

560 Akiya
Yokosuka-shi, Japan
December 1968

PASTORAL COUNSELING–INTRODUCTION AND OVERVIEW

If one studies the history of man, especially that portion which deals with people's reaction to and ability to cope with stress-producing situations, he will find that seeking help from a person or persons invested with some affinity to Deity as a method of easing tension has been the rule rather than the exception.

The religious leader has always considered himself to be a person concerned with the behavior of people. He has always been interested in the individual as a person living with other persons and as a person somehow involved in the cosmic process. He has also been interested in assisting his community in maintaining a state of well-being.

How he has gone about this task may be questioned and, in light of modern science, especially the behavioral sciences, open to scrutiny. Often, the minister is considered to be more vertically orientated than horizontally. Quite often he has lost his sense of perspective timewise and, while dealing with man as a child of eternity, he forgets that he is also a creature of clocks and calendars. To be sure, the religious leader has not always been in the forefront calling for reforms, but where he has been, his was often the "voice of one crying in the wilderness." Sometimes his resistance to things new has stood in the way of inquiry and perhaps progress. But most assuredly, when he was convinced of the value of a thing, he was willing to lay it on the line and become champion of a cause.

While the foregoing may be aptly illustrated historically, especially as it relates to pastoral counseling, such a review would take us too far afield. Furthermore, the history of the "cure of souls" has already been covered and is not germane to this study other than to call attention to two remarks of Freud to the Reverend Pfister.[1] While Freud recognized the value of psychoanalysis as a tool in the hands of the clergy to free suffering humanity, he nevertheless made it quite clear that the two were to remain forever separate. Perhaps if that attitude had been different, one hundred years of alienation between pastoral counseling and psychoanalysis might have been averted. Suffice it to say, pastoral counseling—where the tools and concepts of modern psychology and psychiatry are applied by the minister in working with people in the parish—is now a department of study in almost every divinity school in America. Books on the subject are legion.

When I say that pastoral counseling is the application of the findings and the use of the tools of psychology and/or psychiatry by the minister, several questions are immediately raised, not to mention the emotional reaction aroused in many at the thought of such. In the area of the behavioral sciences, two basic questions are often asked. One is concerned with the compatibility of religion and psychology and/or psychiatry and the other is concerned with the minister's qualifications for using the concepts and methods of the behavioral scientist.

With regards to the first, it would be advantageous if the term *religion* were dropped from the vocabulary or at least, for occasions such as this, if it could be pushed into the background. There are at least two reasons for this observation. One is the ambiguity of the term. One writer has found no less than ninety-six definitions. And however much this may sound like a barb, one has almost as much difficulty finding an accepted and agreed-on definition of psychotherapy. Second, by not using the term, one of the sources of resistance is removed when confronting the "rebel in the abstract." Yet one would certainly not decry the importance of defining terms nor the importance of resistance in working on problems. But any discussion of matters commonly related to religious data often becomes grounds for argu-

mentation which serves no useful purpose. However, one must not forget that both religion and psychology deal almost entirely with metaphysical concepts. They may be mutually exclusive to the detriment of both. And in passing, keep in mind that when one deals with psychoanalysis, he may do so either as a metaphysical concept, as a medical practice or as a both/and proposition. As a metaphysical concept, we are greatly interested in it. As a medical practice, well, that is a part of this lecture.

Now to the task. If we describe our areas of concern and the goals we are trying to achieve, we might be closer together than expected. If we define our concepts and ideas, we may be closer yet than we had anticipated or are willing to admit. If we disclose our methodology, there may be a divergence for some, but a convergence for others. If we delineate our limitations, we may be mutually dependent upon each other. Thus, we might be in a better position to function as a team than many of us have been willing to accept.[2]

Regarding our areas of concern and the goals we are trying to achieve, it seems to me that we are both concerned with the well-being of persons. This may be an oversimplification, but it is minimal enough that none can deny its truth and broad enough that all can agree thereto. How to achieve that goal may be the crux of the matter, for it deals with early recognition of problems, their prevention and/or their cure.

I should like to point out that the minister has a unique position in the community which helps him immensely in this area of mutual concern. First, he is one of the few, perhaps the only one, who does not have to climb the social ladder. Here I can speak from fifteen years of civilian ministerial experience from a small rural parish to a large city parish in the Midwest. He is accepted almost without reservation or at least with a minimum of hesitancy into the social structure of the community—homes, schools, hospitals, jails, civic clubs, business establishments—and is often engaged in extra-church activities and meetings. In the military, there is not much difference. The Cross usually grants him immediate recognition and entry into any activity, officer and enlisted. There are times, however, when I feel there is some reserve by many in the Establishment, but that is something else and is rare. Be that as it may, his acceptance and freedom of movement means he has a rare opportunity to see more people within the framework of their existence than perhaps any other professional. And he sees them in the basic unity of society, the home—and this often means in the confines of their most intimate worlds.[3]

A sampling of problems encountered indicates something of the magnitude of his job. Aside from normal church administrative functions and the problems which exist there (and they are by no means small), he sees people from all walks of life burdened with guilt, shame, suffering from hate, grief, death, loneliness, anxieties, suicidal thoughts, marital problems, pre-marital interests, family problems and conflicts, sexual problems, the storms and stresses of adolescence, ageing, vocational and educational dilemmas, physical illnesses, mental disturbances, emotional difficulties, alcoholism, drug addiction, anti-social behavior, and the tension experienced by people moving into a new community. Thus, he has a public ministry, a pulpit ministry and a private ministry. And while he may not be able to minister to all privately, he can certainly meet a lot of needs and solve a lot of problems by involving himself in what I choose to call therapeutic preaching, by properly educating, training and using his staff. This can be very important. I once pastored a church in which, in addition to the paid staff, there were more than 160 workers in the church school alone. It seems to be a correct observation to say that the minister has the chance to establish a therapeutic community. And that is exactly what we have meant through the years when reference is made to the church as redemptive society. We are not trying to save souls—we are trying to save LIVES!

So much on behalf of his ministry. What about our concepts and ideas? First, I should like to attempt to clear the air of a misconception. Psyche is a word heard quite often in the field of the behavioral sciences. But did you know that the word is almost always translated *soul* in the bible, especially in the New Testament, not to mention the Septuagint, a Greek translation of the Old Testament? Of the 117 times it appears in the Greek New Testament, it means life principle, earthly life, soul or mind, feelings and emotions. Thus, if my business is, as I am often reminded, to save souls, let us be sure the term is being used properly and understandably. The biblical concept from the very outset is that man does not have a soul, he is a soul! And I recognize the importance of making a word mean something specific. But have the behavioral scientists used it any differently than we?

Take one other word: personality. And I mean conceptually. If it means what I think it means in psychological jargon, then the behavioral scientists have used one word to denote a concept the biblical writers have used since the dawn of recorded history: love God with all one's heart, soul, mind and strength. That is, with the whole person. One must also love his neighbors as well as his enemies as he loves himself—not just parts of himself!

Going one step further, I should now like to deal briefly with Freud's Theory of Personality. As you know, the structural aspect of personality has been divided into Id, Ego, Superego and a later entity known as the Ego-Ideal.[4] The Id represents the biologically orientated instincts, drives or impulses. The Superego represents the prohibitions, codes of conduct, rules and regulations received from the family and community. The Ego is the self and its interpretations of life. Dynamically speaking, the Id is motivated by need fulfillment or wish fulfillment; the Superego seeks to inhibit by holding up ideal standards; and the Ego seeks to reconcile the impulses of the Id with the restrictions of the Superego on a reality basis or in consonance with the world of reality.

As I mentioned, the Ego-Ideal came later in Freud's thinking and was left undeveloped as a separate entity from the Superego except by some of his students: Reik, Nunberg, Deutsch, de Groot, *et al.*[5] Freud seems to have always identified the Superego and the Ego-Ideal as one. Be that as it may, the Ego-Ideal is representative of the ideal person which the person aspires to be and is separated from the Superego which now represents strict ethical demands.

Now, is there a comparable concept in theology or biblical thought? I think there is and it might be called a Theology of Persons. I base my judgment on a study of the experience of St. Paul related in Romans 7:14-25.[6] As far as is known, no one has looked at that experience in view of the foregoing analytic concepts. When this is done, however, a whole new area of thought is opened. Paul uses the term *sarks* (flesh) as opposed to *soma* (body) to denote a source of internalized difficulty. And it sounds as though he is referring to something that is biologically orientated with certain psychological overtones. Then he talks about a kind of law (or ruling principle) which prohibits him from expressing the demands of *sarks*. This law or ethical standard seems to be based upon something congenital, derived from natural law (or an evolved ethical standard), fortified by the Law (or Ten Commandments), which may be superseded or have superimposed upon it an even greater law: the Law of the Spirit. Yet, he seems to be saying exactly the same thing Freud said about the Superego and its development. Thus, his experience can be reduced to the inner stress caused by *sarks* (Id?) which is about to get out of control but is held in check by the impossible demands of the internalized Law (Superego?) and the Ego (same in both Paul and Freud) is unable to reconcile the conflict. Well, what do you do until an Ego comes along which is strong enough to stand on its own two feet? Paul simply (?) found an ideal or a significant person with whom he could identify and made or formed an alliance with him. From this relationship with the Divine *Imago* (Ego-Ideal?), he gained the strength necessary to do what he believed he should do. Thereafter, we have no further problems with this particular conflict.

Leaving this for the moment, let us now talk briefly about certain limitations.[7] First, there is the limitation imposed by the organicity of a particular problem. There should be no doubt in the minister's mind about the medical problem so defined. Yet, you and I know the assistance the minister can offer the suffering patient under the circumstances. And while I do not wish to go off on a tangent, I contend that both the doctor and the minister should leave the door open to the possibility of a "miracle." At least, where an organic disorder occurs.

A second limitation, at least between the medically trained psychotherapist (I make no distinction between the pastoral counselor and any other *non*medical therapist) and pastoral counselor, may be aptly illustrated in a comment made by my older son when he was age four. On the morning after I received my doctorate, he asked my wife what kind of a doctor I was. Apparently he had asked if I was like our pediatrician. Relieved that I was not, he came into the room where I was and said, with a note of triumph and relief, "Ha, ha, ha! You're a doctor but you can't give shots."

In closing, I would remind you there are now more than nine thousand ministers who have completed training in mental hospitals and there will be more to follow.[8] What then is the difference? Succinctly, counseling is psychotherapy as carried on by the minister, and psychotherapy is counseling as practiced by the psychiatrist and/or psychologist.

NOTES AND BIBLIOGRAPHY

LECTURE I
1. In 1909, Freud wrote the Reverend Oscar Pfister:

> In itself, psychoanalysis is neither religious nor the opposite, but an impartial instrument which can serve the clergy as well as the laity when it is used only to free suffering people ... I have never thought of the extraordinary help the psychoanalytic method can be in pastoral work, probably because wicked heretics like us are far away from the circle.

In 1918, he wrote again:

> From a therapeutic point of view, I can only envy your opportunity of bringing about sublimation into religion. But the beauty of religion assuredly has no place in psychoanalysis. Naturally, our paths diverge here, and it can stay at that.

Quoted by Reissner, "Religion and Psycho-Therapy."

2. Leslie has proposed the following stages of development in the relationship between psychotherapy and pastoral counseling:

> (1) Open hostility between the psychotherapist as a man of science and the pastoral counselor as a man of religion.
> (2) A kind of capitulation of the minister to psychiatry with ministers bowing in obeisance before the new found wisdom of psychoanalytic theory. Referrals were usually one way.
> (3) The two are now approaching the level where the two professional groups can meet without defensiveness to the mutual advantage of both.

See "Psychotherapist and Pastoral Counselors," Leslie,
In 1965, the Committee on Religion and Psychiatry of the

American Psychiatric Association published the following report on the work and function of the Committee:

> (1) Function as a medium of communication between psychiatrist and religious leaders.
> (2) Develop programs for the use of the pastoral counselors as mental health assistants.
> (3) Help to provide mental health training in seminaries.
> (4) Work toward the training of medical students and residents in psychiatry in the use of pastoral counselors.
> (5) Stimulate interest among psychiatrists in cooperating with and assisting church groups.
> (6) Invite the collaboration of clergymen in programs in which they and psychiatrists agree fully or in part.

From "Religion and Mental Health" by Blain.

3. With regards to the role of the minister, Dr. Steinzor wrote the following:

> There is no profession in our community more complicated and thus more difficult to pursue with relative equilibrium than the ministry. The roles the clergyman is expected to fulfill from administrator, fund raiser, preacher, through pastor to the living and the dying, etc.; the public's highly ambivalent attitudes toward him; and the variety of interpretations of the biblical tradition available to him are among the significant social pressures he experiences. The very presence of the dialogue between theology and the behavioral sciences is only one manifestation of the pressure on the minister to keep abreast of progress and rapid change while he is also expected to invoke the voice of the past centuries ... In the community, *it is the minister who is the therapist when he raises to higher levels of consciousness the ways in which the individual in his community suffers because of the ways the community reveals in its institutions its blindness to the rule of love and justice.* [Emphasis added]

From the article, "Social Therapist" by Steinzor.

In regards to the relationship between religion and psychotherapy, Dr. Reissner wrote:

> The marriage of the medical and the spiritual treatment of illness has a long and honorable history. The word "salvation"

characterizes the highest ideal of Christian striving, is rooted in Greek and Latin medical terminology, and the words for "healer" in Greek and Latin are semantically identical with it. This is not to say that the healing of mental illness has always been performed by combining medical arts with religious conceptions. But *history shows that when the church has been weakened by internal strife, say, or by stubborn opposition to science, it has often relinquished the domain of the care of the sick mind.* [Emphasis added]

From "Religion and Psychotherapy" by Reissner.

4. This is enlarged upon in Chapter II, but see:
Freud, *Group Psychology,* pp. 690c-691c.
———, *Ego and Id,* pp. 706b-707c, 715a-b.
———, *Introductory Lectures,* p. 831b.
———, *Moses,* pp. 148ff.
———, *Lay-Analysis,* pp. 17ff.

5. Deutsch, *Character Types,* pp. 330ff.
Lampl-de Groote, *Development of the Mind.*
Nunberg, *Psychoanalysis.*
Reik, *Love and Lust.*

6. These notions are enlarged upon in Chapter III. Since we are dealing with a matter of grave psychological as well as theological concern, it seems important to observe a serious conflict between the religious sector and psychoanalysis. I refer to the theory and handling of repressed material. In this area, the church by and large has been on the side of suppression while Freud from a psychological point of view has praised the theological posture of St. Paul. Said he, *Paul "has done us a great service by accenting the return of the repressed."* [Emphasis added] See *Moses,* p. 109ff.

7. Dr. Folles has observed that

> because the majority [of people in distress] turn to their clergyman during the first time of trouble, it is the responsibility of the religious leader to differentiate among those who can be helped by pastoral care, those who need a more specialized type of pastoral counseling, and those in serious distress who require professional psychiatric care.

From "Religion in Mental Health." Folles.
Dr. Folles further stated with regards to the limitations of both the psychiatrist and the clergyman that

> the Psychiatrist and Clergyman must understand each other's role and each must understand the limitation of his own. When a religious person is suffering deep emotional consequence of real guilt, a good psychiatrist will send him to his clergyman. Chances are he is seeking forgiveness and not psychoanalysis. Conversely, if the distress is brought on by imagined guilt that has no basis in reality, a good clergyman will send him to a psychiatrist. [Ibid.]

8. Attention is called to the fact that Freud rued the day when psychoanalysis became the sole province of the medical practitioner. See Freud, *Lay-Analysis*, Editor's preface, pp. 53ff, Chapters V, VI, VII and Postscript.

In addition, the following by Bruder is of interest:

> More and more hospital administrators are encouraging the additions to their staffs of clinically trained Chaplains. They do this not only to provide a ministry sensitized to the needs of their patients, but through the Chaplain's clinical training programs to make available additional friendly supportive professional personnel who take an interest in their patients. Hence there is a direct gain to the hospital and to patients as more and more seminarians and ministers venture through the stone walls of fear, suspicion, misunderstanding, and stigma which still surrounds all too many of modern mental hospitals.

Bruder, "Minister and Mental Health."

For a more definitive study on this matter, my paper on "The Chaplain and the Community Psychiatrist" which was given and well received by the Journal Club, Neuro-Psychiatric Service, U. S. Naval Hospital, Oakland, California, 1965, proposes a workable relationship. And, I might add, my experiences in both the civilian and military communities proves the possibility and value of a working relationship.

A THEORY OF PERSONALITY – FREUD

Ladies and gentlemen, it is indeed a pleasure to discuss Freud's Theory of Personality. My interest in the subject has been more than academic; it has been clinical as well. I am not a psychiatrist and I do not feel it is necessary to be one in order to show one's interest in Freud's theory in particular or psychoanalysis in general. However, there are certain limitations which must be readily accepted in dealing, not so much with psychoanalysis, as with psychiatry in which certain medical and legal problems are presupposed. Nevertheless, there are, within the fields of both psychoanalysis and psychiatry, concepts and practices which the laity can use and use beneficially and satisfactorily. But the minister is more than a layman. He is a professional and his profession, historically and traditionally, has qualified him as a student of behavior. As a behavioral scientist, and I do not use that term unadvisedly, he has an interest in any theory or methodology which will help him to understand and deal with those in his care (Vide Lecture I, esp. note 3).

Now to the task. It is a truism that Freud gave us a theory of personality and a methodology by which to deal with certain problems arising out of a person's response to his environment and the conflicts one often experiences due to various reasons. In this, Freud was a pioneer. His was the first effort toward a systematic study of persons psychologically. It is unfortunate that he died before he could complete the task and refine his work into a more definitive system. Perhaps the nearest he came to such was in his *New Introductory Lectures on Psychoanalysis.*[1] It has fallen to his disciples through continued study and clinical observation to try to enlarge upon those formulations.

While there are many popular and technical books written to explain the theory and practice of psychoanalysis, Rapport[2] has provided a very fine frame of reference which seems to be most practical and beneficial for a study of Freud's theory. His structural mode has been refined in the *American Handbook of Psychiatry*.[3] It is adapted for this presentation.

First a word about purpose. I am interested in the basic formulation of Freud's Structure of Personality as it may or may not relate to what I am calling a Theology of Persons as introduced by St. Paul in his Epistle to the Romans, especially in chapter seven, verses fourteen through twenty-five. I believe that once Freud's notions are dealt with *conceptually,* and once some understanding is gained of what St. Paul seems to be describing based upon his own self-observation as it relates to his personal experience, that experience and the formulations of Freud may be closely related. Furthermore, St. Paul may have been struggling with a concept not unlike Freud's. If that is true, it raises an interesting side issue: why has Freud been so widely accepted and St. Paul neglected if not rejected? Could it be the religious flavor? One is reminded that Freud was not kindly disposed to religion.

Be that as it may, there are six main divisions in the analytic system:

        Structural
        Topographic
        Genetic
        Economic
        Dynamic
        Therapeutic

In historical development, the topographic came first. This division related to Freud's first attempt to structure the psyche at three levels: conscious, preconscious and unconscious.[4] As in the lay of the land, so in the psyche, there are things in the open and accessible; others are located at or near the surface and these are accessible with some degree of effort; but others are well below the surface and must be excavated. Freud used the analogy of an iceberg to describe this notion. Topographic, then, refers to the lay of the mind. It is more aptly called levels of response or levels of awareness.

Freud[5] later observed that "levels of awareness" was not sufficient to explain a more definitive type of response which he was observing. At each of these levels, certain responses were being witnessed which were to be further identified in more basic terms. For example, certain individuals were struggling with ideas, notions or desires which seemed to be forbidden, not so much by the social milieu, as by some internal inhibiting force. For some reason, the person was unable to reconcile the conflict thus created. The desire he named Id; the forbidding force he called Superego; and, the reconciling factor which seemed to be lacking was an autonomous self he designated Ego. The person caught in this internal struggle has developed no value judgments of his own, or else he is afraid to exert his will against the value judgments he has learned as a child, which are now a part of him and which exist to some extent, in the social context of his existence. Id, Ego and Superego compose the structural division.

Now, before enlarging upon these notions, a word should be said regarding a popular misconception about the Id. Id is more than mere sexuality.[6] True, Freud did see many of his patients struggling with sexual problems or at least with problems of a sexual nature. This sexual flavoring he called eros. However, eros is more definitive than sexuality and Id is more than a sexual orientation. Eros refers to love in its larger meaning and Id refers to the basic drives, needs or instincts of the organism. He also observed in his patients a certain trend or drive toward what appeared to be a "drive toward destruction." He later labeled this drive thanatos: the death instinct. Eros and thanatos with the notion of the libido or energy compose the dynamic aspect of analytic theory.

In the course of his work, Freud observed that certain behavior took on the characteristics of activity associated with certain early developmental stages in childhood. For example, it can be observed that children at various stages of growth do show a particular interest in certain areas and activities of their bodies. They also become interested in what is happening within their environment as it begins to expand and take in more people. Because the content of the activity seemed obvious, Freud called these stages oral, anal, phallic (latency), and genital.[7] But what caught his attention was not the activity of children, but the fact that certain of his patients seemed to be re-living or had become fixated at these stages. It seemed they had regressed under stress to a former way of handling their conflicts. These concepts make up the genetic division and often refer to the history of psychiatric development. The oedipal complex falls within this area.

Since, as Freud supposed, the organism is always seeking satisfaction, gratification or tension reduction,[8] there is the "press for action." He believed this drive would be executed in the most effective manner and with the greatest conservation of energy possible. This has been labeled the economic division.

While the therapeutic division is of great interest, it is not germane to this work.

Having given you a quick, if not overly simplified, look at Freud's theory, let us look in more detail at the structural division. First, concerning the Id.[9] It seems natural that Freud, being a neurologist and greatly influenced by Darwin's Theory of Evolution, should conceive of the Id as being primarily biologically orientated. For example, sexuality, hunger and elimination of waste are basically biologically centered. Pleasure and pain, if not felt physically, are usually referred to in physical terms. Life in general as well as in particular can be more easily understood in biological terminology than in philosophical or theological jargon. Death itself is the termination of biological processes. The concept of the libido or energy can be better understood physic-ally. These drives, the press for release of tension or urges to activity, desires, needs, or, as Freud called them, instincts, are labeled Id. It is to be understood as the psychic representation of biologically orientated drives. It is described as unprincipled, nonmoral, illogical, pleasure motivated. It aims primarily at gratification and demands immediate attention. It is congenital: that is, it comes with birth. It may be referred to as the raw material out of which the person develops, if not physically, certainly psychologically. It is unable to distinguish between the real and the not-real. To make this distinction, Ego and Superego develop.

Concerning the Ego. In his book, *The Problem of Lay-Analysis*,[10] Freud offered the following observations regarding the function of the Ego (or the autonomous self, if we may make such an interpretation). The Id, uncontrolled and demanding satisfaction, needs some guiding hand to help in its quest for satisfaction or gratification in accordance with the real world. For example, the infant is a dynamic organism of self-concerned activity. He is organismic-centered as opposed to Ego-centered. Since no Ego has as yet developed, the infant cannot be egocentric. However, he soon begins a series of learned behavior. He learns by crying that he will be fed, have his diaper changed, or be fondled. By sneezing, he communicates, among other things, that he is either in a draft or has lint on his nose. Freud considered this activity to be reflexive, initially unlearned and inborn, therefore, instinctual. The infant also learns from or through the sensorium certain impressions of how needs are satisfied, thwarted or postponed. Here a struggle ensues between the organism and his environment which is largely attended by the mother. Slowly, he begins to organize his mental processes and develops a world within. He learns to perceive objects, to make distinctions in stimuli. He acquires ways and means to adapt to his environment and learns other ways of achieving gratification. He learns to control instinctual strivings and the discharge of energy in conformity to the standards set by his environment: social and natural. In short, he develops some inner control device or Ego as Freud called it. The function of the Ego is to mediate between the world and the Id. It tries to help the Id comply with external demands and to discharge its energy according to the standards set by the outside world. Thus, its primary function is to aid the Id in the control of instincts in keeping with the well-being of the organism and society. In other words, it tries to strike a balance and maintain harmony within (intra-psychic) and without (extra-psychic) the individual.

Now, with regards to the Superego.[11] As one can see, the Id demands some means of control and the Ego needs some standard by which to exercise its power of control. The Superego provides these standards. First, they are externally imposed and are the standards, values, morals or principles derived from the parents and the environment of home. Later, these are expanded to include the injunctions and prohibitions of other authorities. The Superego contains what is expected of the higher nature of man. It represents and seeks to impose ideal behavior. Through identification and introjection, the individual begins to develop his own moral system or superego by incorporating the values of his society into his own *psyche.*

More succinctly, the Id, unprincipled or untamed, seeks gratification at will. The Superego inhibits or prohibits this undisciplined behavior, or wish to behave, by imposing rigid, idealistic standards. It is the Ego's task to reconcile the difference in accordance with the reality principle. Should the Ego falter or capitulate to either the Id or the Superego, pathology ensues. Dissolution of this problem is the task of therapy.

Consider the Ego-ideal.[12] At first, Freud identified the Ego-ideal (the ideal person) with the Superego. It is not clear whether he actually made a distinction between the two. Perhaps this was due to his death (he never refined his concepts into a more definitive system as some theorists have since). However, his students have gone on to delineate between the Superego and Ego-ideal (See Chapter I, Note 5). Basically, the Superego became identified with moral systems and the Ego-ideal became identified with the ideal person: the person one would most like to be or be like. This distinction will be important in our study of St. Paul and especially so in our discussions on guilt and shame (Chapters IV and V).

Please keep in mind that the structural (Id, Ego, Superego/Ego-ideal) is an interrelated, interacting, intertwined system and its concepts are interlaced with the topographic system (conscious, preconscious and unconscious). As a matter of fact, Freud often identified the Superego with the conscience, but later gave to it (conscience) the function of censor of the Id in the service of the Superego while at the same time punitively attacking the Ego for not doing its job.

I trust enough has now been said to help us in our study St. Paul, to which we now turn our attention.

NOTES AND BIBLIOGRAPHY

Lecture II
1. Freud, *Introductory Lectures.*
2. Rapport, *Collected Papers,* Chapter 14.
3. *American Handbook of Psychiatry,* p. 1400ff.
4. Freud, *Ego and Id,* p. 697b-98c and elsewhere.
5. *Ibid.,* p. 699a-ff.
6. On Id and the Instincts, see *Introduction to Psychoanalysis,* Lecture 21; *Lay-Analysis,* p. 35ff; *Ego and Id,* p. 702a-ff; *Pleasure Principle,* Para. 5.
7. On Libido, see *Origin and Development,* p. 16; *Introduction to Psychoanalysis,* Lecture 26; *Lay-Analysis,* p. 40; *Ego and Id,* p. 708ff.
On Development and Repression, *Introduction to Psychoanalysis,* Lecture 22; *Lay-Analysis,* p. 44.
8. On Oedipus Complex, *Origin and Development,* pp. 17f; *Dreams,* pp. 242-8; *Ego and Id,* p. 703ff, and elsewhere.
On Renunciation and Gratification, *Lay-Analysis,* p. 85ff; *Moses,* p. 148ff.
9. *Lay-Analysis,* pp. 17, 25, 29; *Ego and Id,* pp. 201d-ff.
10. *Ibid.,* p. 28ff; *Ego and Id,* pp. 702a-ff; *Moses,* p. 148ff.
11. On the Superego, *On Narcissim,* p. 399ff; *Group Psychology,* p. 664ff; *Ego and Id,* pp. 703ff, 707ff; *Lay-Analysis,* p. 59ff.
12. On the Ego-Ideal, *Ego and Id,* p. 703ff; *Moses,* p. 148ff.

A THEOLOGY OF PERSONS – ST. PAUL

Ladies and gentlemen, as far as is known, no one has as yet considered the experience of St. Paul in Romans 7:14-25 from a psychological point of view. As far as is known, no one has undertaken a study or made attempts to develop a theology of personality beyond that which is customarily handled in that subdivision of theology called anthropology or the study of man from a biblical and theological point of view. As far as is known, no one has looked at the experience of St. Paul from the structural, topographical and dynamic divisions of analytic thought. These we will atttempt today. The study is suggestive and exploratory only.

Before proceeding with our study, I should like to share an experience. During my third year of clinical training, I presented a paper to the Journal Club of a large neuropsychiatric service. My opening remark was, "Having a theology which is psychologically sound and analytically orientated, I should like to discuss. . . . " I had hoped for a challenge from the floor by at least one of the several psychiatrists, psychologists or social workers present. None was forthcoming, although several people looked at each other and two psychologists paired and began a private conversation. After the meeting, a psychologist stated that he had started to question my statement on the grounds that he had studied theology and had been unable to see any relationship between it and the behavioral sciences.

Since he had opened the door, I felt we could talk further about the matter. I proceeded to present what is to be discussed here today. After sketching in brief what I had hoped to do at the club, he said, "Hmmm (note the professional tone in that expression), I'd never thought of that." Subsequently, when I diagramatically presented the structural division of analytic theory and a similar diagram of what I thought St. Paul was describing, a clinical psychologist, who taught in a nearby seminary, said, "By golly, I'd never thought of that in those terms before." When I presented the same to a contemporary who had spent twenty years as a chaplain in various hospitals and who was assigned to provide chaplain N-P trainees with assistance, he said, "Gee, all you guys want to talk about is theology."

Strange, indeed if not ironic, that he responded differently than the two psychologists? Well, these have been typical responses. However, a number of my colleagues have encouraged me to develop my thoughts along this line and I have done so here, formally, for the first time.

As you know, Romans has been one of the more difficult epistles to understand. It is profound in depth and breadth. In it, the writer struggles with the sin problem (individually and collectively), Law-type ethics, the relationship between Christ and the Law, Spirit-type ethics, the problem of the Jew as a member of an elect race, and endless social problems. The seventh chapter of Romans falls within that section in which the author struggles with the problem of sin, its relation to the Law and its demands for right conduct.

It is interesting to note that the author changes to first person in describing this experience. It is *his* experience. And, one might add, it is a very profound observation or self analysis, if that term may be used. He finds himself in what is obviously an intra-psychic dilemma. It is no less extra-psychic because of the social implications. He is caught in a struggle between value systems and personal loyalty. To accept one means to reject the other. But it is more than that. He is also caught between the demands of his lower nature as dominated by the sin-principle and a Law-type ethic which demands right conduct beyond his capability. He knows what is expected of him; yet, he is incapable of doing it. He wants to do what is required by the ethos of his race and his God;

but, he cannot. He aspired to conform to the high demands of a Law ethic but finds his efforts thwarted or sabotaged by a much stronger element within his person: the Law cannot control fleshly desires and the Law appears to be inferior to Christ's way which is now threatening intrusion. He despairs until he relates to the Christ.

Once this decision or commitment is made, he finds the Law supplanted and another ethic either superimposed upon the old system or one which has superseded and abrogated it. Thereafter, however, a new struggle ensues: not the struggle to conform to the values of his ethnic heritage, but to identify with a significant person. It is the difference between being an obedient citizen and living by the values of his race (a religiously orientated race incidently), or becoming a loyal subject and doing what is expected by a significant person. Paul chooses the latter and in so doing jeopardized his relationship with his people. His conflicts are both intra- and extra-psychic.

Parenthetically, I cannot emphasize enough the difference between a Law-type ethic and that which is generated by a significant person. I hope to demonstrate this in the lectures on guilt and shame.

And now the problem as St. Paul seems to be describing it. It is a conflict between two intra-psychic forces: the flesh or, to use the Greek, *sarks* and the Law or *nomos*. In addition, it is a struggle with an extra-psychic force also: the demands of Christ now threatening internalization by the Spirit. Consider how this relates to a structure of personality.

However, before proceeding, I must relate another experience. During my doctoral studies, a fellow classmate presented a paper on *sarks* in a seminar on New Testament theology. One of his conclusions was that there seemed to be "no specific doctrine of *sarks* to be found in the New Testament." Perhaps had he looked at *sarks* as it was used in the Greco-Roman world or as a part of the personality structure of man, he might have concluded otherwise. Furthermore, since theology has not given us a Theology of Persons, pastoral counseling is without orientation. And I might add, pastoral psychology has not given us a psychology of personality either. Up to this time, it has adopted without considering the consequence the theory and practice of psychological counseling. It has a method without a frame of reference or a theory.

Why is it important to have a theory or, as I am calling it, a theology of persons? Simply because counseling is the extension of that theology into a therapeutic situation. Every therapeutic system has its own theoretical constructs which guide the therapeutic process. Pastoral counseling has either tried to impose the methodology of these systems upon theology or else has replaced its theology with the various theories of personality as indicated by the system it embraces (For example: Freudian, Neo-Freudian, Jungian, Rogerian, etc.). One needs only to refer to any number of books on pastoral counseling and ask, how many of them start with a clearly defined Theology or Psychology of Persons?

Now the term *sarks* (sarkikos, sarkinos, sarkos). It is interesting to note that it is used approximately twenty-four times in the Gospels and Acts and some seventy-nine times in the Pauline epistles. In the Pauline usage, twenty-eight are in Romans, eighteen of which are in Romans, chapters seven and eight. Of these eighteen times, fifteen are in Romans, chapter eight where *sarks* takes on a new struggle, not with the Law or *nomos,* but with the Spirit or *pneumatos,* indicating we believe that the struggle with an impersonal ethic such as the Law is not as great as that between two people.

Of the remaining times the term is used in Paul's writing, fourteen appear in Galatians, twenty-two in the Corinthian letters with the remaining twenty-two in the other letters. This is indeed interesting. All these epistles were to people who lived in the Greco-Roman world. This may show at least two things: Paul's orientation to Greek philosophy where the term is used extensively by Socrates or Plato and Aristotle and the fact that the term was in general use in the Greco-Roman world as opposed to the Jewish world. Incidentally, this would hold true also for the Gospels in which the term is used almost exclusively in the Gospel of St. John which was written, so we believe, primarily to Greek audiences. Thus, it is a Greek and not a Jewish concept.

Sarks is to be distinguished from body or *soma* which signifies an organism—a system of skillfully combined parts (Cf. Col. 2:11). *Sarks* is a part of *soma* but *soma* is not *sarks*. They are distinct, yet *soma* includes *sarks*. *Soma* is the totality of a person's physical makeup; *sarks* is only a part thereof. *Sarks* refers to flesh as opposed to bone. *Sarks* includes tissue, blood, nerves and the coverings of the body. But it is more!

Occasionally, *sarks* is translated carnal in the King James version. However, this is a carry-over from the Vulgate where the Latin words *carnelis* and *carneus* are transliterated carnal. Epicuris believed *carnelis* and *carneus* were the bearers of sinful feelings and desires as well as the means of sensual enjoyment. Luther[2] stressed that "flesh was not flesh as we commonly think of flesh" (as we normally think of skin, tissue and blood) and leaves the impression that it is the source of the base or lower, sensual appetites of man. Arndt and Gingrich refer to it as the source of sexual urges and state that it may be considered a standard by which to live. That is, it identifies a person who, like the animal (?), lives merely by physical appetites: to be taken as including all the desires, urges and/or instincts.

However, the word goes back beyond the Latin. Socrates distinguished between flesh *(sarks)* and soul *(psyche).*[3] He believed *sarks* was the prison house of the *psyche* and that the *psyche* would never gain its goal in life so long as it was controlled, held in prison or dominated by *sarks* with its needs and desires! Since this concept was carried over into Latin thought, and since Paul wrote prior to the time of the Vulgate, we may conclude that he was writing under this influence and was using the concept accordingly. Since Freud was greatly influenced by Paul, was he unconsciously receptive to this notion (see Chapter I, note 6)?

Now, in conclusion on *sarks*. Paul seems to be saying (perhaps I should say, it *sounds like* he is saying) that the flesh is the seat and source of certain desires which dog one's feet and interferes with his attaining a higher goal. But more specifically, it is the means whereby the sin-principle or *hamartia* (instinct?) gets the upper hold on man and drives him to rebel against authority as represented by the Law. It perverts normal desires and causes even the best of intentions to be thwarted and deterred. That it is biologically orientated goes without saying. However, it is not the flesh or *sarks* as such which is uncontrolled. *It is the fact that it becomes the medium by which the sin-instinct takes charge!* In a sense, *hamartia* is as great as *zooai* or life-principle (instinct?). Because of it *(hamartia),* man is doomed to failure unless he can find an authority which is capable of controlling, if not eradicating it from his nature (See II Cor. 4:11).

I trust I am not reading too much into *sarks* or Paul when I say that it *sounds* very much like the Id concept of Freud. I trust, also, that I am not stretching the point when I say that *zooai* (life-instinct) equates eros (love-instinct) and *hamartia* (sin-instinct) equates thanatos (death-instinct).

I should like now to consider the term Ego. Here there is not much of a struggle with basic words since Ego is the same in both Greek and Latin. However, philologically, the Latin has carried the word over from the Greek. Ego is translated *I* some twenty-two times in this particular section of Romans (7:14-25). It is to be distinguished from *sarks* although it is related to it (7:14). Incidentally, Freud stated that in normal people there may be no difference between Ego and Id.[4] Now, by itself, the Ego is ineffective against the sin-instinct (Romans 7:17). It recognizes the right as opposed to the wrong but is not able to act in favor of the good (7:15, 16, 19). That is, it has no strength or energy of its own. Ego has the best of intentions (7:15, 19). It agrees that the *nomos*—the standard which regulates behavior—is right (7:16, 22). But even here, the Ego is not strong enough to exert itself: the Law is right but it cannot be kept. It is too demanding and too idealistic (7:21).

At this point, another faculty is added: mind or *noos* (7:22, 23, 25). *Noos* refers to that faculty which thinks, reasons and assists in making decisions. As *sarks* identifies with the sin-instinct (7:25) and leaves one in the grips of a terrible and seemingly unresolvable conflict, *noos* identifies with the good. Well, what does one do until an Ego, strong enough to absolve the conflict, comes along? Doesn't it *sound* as though St. Paul expected the Ego to function much in the same manner as did Freud?

Now, an important question: what is the other law he refers to in 7:23? Is this referring to conscience? One is reminded that conscience or *sunidesis* played an important part in Paul's life (Vide, Romans 2:15; 9:1; 1 Timothy 3:9; 2 Timothy 4:2; Titus 1:15 and elsewhere). Certainly there is a distinction to be made between *noos* and *sunidesis*. It seems *sunidesis* refers to an emotional kind of knowledge while *noos* refers to cognition. Thus, *sunidesis* may refer to the system consciousness. But it seems Paul is using *noos* as an appendage to the Ego. Thus, while *sunidesis* assists the Superego, *noos* works in the service of the Ego. This may be a significant addition to the structural division.

We turn our attention now to *nomos* or law. It goes without saying that this represents the authority by which conduct is regulated. It seems evident that it is both intra- and extra-psychic. And it is indeed interesting that Paul gives a remarkable account of how this part of the personality is formulated. From Romans 2:14, 15, two important statements are made. First, man is endowed from birth with the faculty which predisposes him to ethical actions. Upon this congenital factor, man, left to himself, evolves or goes about to establish (in his own prelogical fashion) certain standards by which to regulate the behavior of his ethnic group. Moffatt[5] translates "when the Gentiles do my nature" to read, "who obey the law instinctively." Law in this sense is the ethical principles inherent in the world as opposed to but supportive of Law (the Ten Commandments). This is sometimes referred to as the natural moral law.

Now, if one perchance is born into the elect race, he may be considered heir to the Divine Law or Ten Commandments *(entolai)* which is more definitive than the evolved ethic (Romans 3:1, 2; 9:4; Exodus 20). However, within this group as in the non-elect, interpretations, customs and traditions are handed down and may be more binding than the original law or Law intended (Vide, the *Talmud* or the Rabbinical interpretations of the Law). However, in Romans 8, he introduces a fifth level: the law of the Spirit or *nomos tou pneumatos.* In New Testament language, the Spirit refers to the invisible presence of God. As Paul uses it, it is either superimposed upon the other levels, or else, and he argues very strongly for this, it supersedes and abrogates all the others except in that it relates to the congenital foundation and is therefore not a foreign or extraneous force. Among other things, this means that a new authority system is now in force: the personal presence of God regent within the person in the person of the Holy Spirit. I shan't go further with that at this time. Suffice it to say, for a study in the psychological reactions to shifts in authority structures (in a gross form), I can only refer you to a very fine book: *The Three Christs of Ypsilanti.*[6]

In conclusion, I should like to make the following summation and diagram. As long as *sarks* and *nomos* are in conflict, the Ego is unable to function due to some inherent weakness. However, Paul, in desperation, sees the value of a significant person and identifies with him. Jesus was that person. He is the person whom Paul would not only like to be but the one who becomes the object of his worship and devotion. The Ego gains strength from this relationship through the indwelling Spirit and is now able to function. Jesus, the Divine *Imago*, equates the Ego-ideal.

In Freud's thinking, there could be conflict between the Superego and the Ego-ideal. For example, the person in authority may say, "don't do as I do, but do as I say." This may frustrate the Ego. However, in Christian theology, the Spirit and the Divine *Imago* are in agreement. As long as the Law reigned, there was conflict between it and the demands of Christ. Paul argues that the Spirit takes the place of the Law as a standard of ethical behavior. It agrees with the Divine *Imago* since both are personal and representative of the same Divine Person. The Ego identifies with the Divine *Imago* and finds strength from both the *nomos* of the Spirit and the Christ: the authority system is now consistent and in agreement. Even if the old nature condemns, God (the Supreme Authority) is greater than that nature (I John 3:20). The Spirit takes control of *sarks*, holds it in check or else releases the desire in accordance with the practice of the Divine *Imago*. Any exacerbation of the sin-instinct *(hamartia)* is not the job of the Ego but of the Spirit.

Now, this gets into the area of Christian conversion and I shan't go further with the notion. However, I will refer you to a very interesting book written by an English psychiatrist, Ernest White, *The Christian Life and the Unconscious*.[7] He believes, as do many, that Christian conversion affects the unconscious. For a good description of this from a personal experience, you are referred to St. Paul's personal apprisal of what happened to him as recorded in 2 Corinthians 4:7-5:10.

I should like now to diagram these two trains of thought.

Freud's Structure	St. Paul
Superego (Conscience)	*Nomos* *(Sunidesis)*
Ego-Ideal	Divine *Imago*
Ego	Ego *(Noos)*
Id Eros Thanatos	*Sarks* *Zooai* *Hamartia*

Plate 1

As one can see, if diagrammed like this, there is similarity. And, as I said at the outset, it is suggestive and exploratory only.

NOTES AND BIBLIOGRAPHY

Lecture III

1. Concerning the various biblical and theological discussions of Romans 7:14-25, reference may be made to any number of commentaries on Romans. The following are suggestive:
Barth, *Commentary*.
Brunner, *Letter to Romans*.
Godet, *Epistle to Romans*.
Lenski, *St. Paul's Epistle to Romans*.
Denny, *Epistle to Romans* and *Expositor's Greek Testament*.

2. As quoted by Arndt and Gingrich, *Lexicon*.
3. Plato, "Phaedo," *Dialogues*, Vol. I, pp. 446-51.
4. Freud, *Lay-Analysis*, p. 27.
5. Moffatt, *Bible*.
6. Rokeach, *Three Christs*.
7. White, *Christian Life*.

"OUT, DAMNED SPOT! OUT!" A STUDY IN GUILT

Ladies and gentlemen, in the next two lectures, the subjects of guilt and shame are to be discussed. It will be no easy task for a number of reasons. Generally speaking, no distinction is made between the two. This is due in part to the fact that shame is not discussed by Freud[1] nor does it appear in later analytic writings (at least not until recently). Second, Piers and Singer[2] have made, as far as we know, the first useful distinction between the two; yet, not too many people are familiar with their work. Third, there is a possibility that Freud meant the notion of shame when he briefly mentioned inferiority in *New Introductory Lectures,* Lecture 31.[3] Fourth, Freud may have been handicapped by the ethic of his heritage. The Jewish ethic has always been a law-type ethic. The traditional notion is that "justice will triumph." Then, too, one must not forget that Freud wrote against the backdrop of a Catholic dominated community where legalism and guilt played a large part. Finally, the subject is difficult to handle because the distinction can be made more easily if the two concepts are dealt with simultaneously. Thus, if allusions are made to shame in this lecture, no apology is offered. The stage will be set for the following discourse.[4]

Freud, you will recall, referred often to a sense of guilt or a feeling of guilt.[5] Mowrer[6] has taken him to task by stating that the reason a person feels guilt is precisely because he is guilty. We may have occasion to return to this idea later. However, we are now interested in the origin and development of this sense of guilt as Freud conceived it. He believed it originated in the earliest years of childhood arising out of the conflict between the child and the parents. This struggle he defined as the Oedipal Complex after *Oedipus Rex.*[7]

Before proceeding, may I suggest that if you have not read this tragedy, you are urged to do so—as well as some of the other Greek plays. It is amazing how much of these is carried over into New Testament thought. In addition to *sarks* and *psyche*, as mentioned in the last lecture, your attention is invited to a statement in *The Seven Against Thebes* as a further example, "The field of sin is reaped with a harvest of death."[8]

Oedipus Rex is the drama of a man who murdered his father and married his mother. Freud believed the early struggle of the child was a struggle to possess one or the other of the parents depending upon the sex of the child. The boy desires the mother and the girl, the father. For the boy, the father stands in the way. For the girl, the mother is an obstacle. Of course, we are shocked at the implied sexuality attributed to this involvement and no less so of the murder impulse. Freud claimed this to be precisely the point of the problem.[9] Incest and murder are not only forbidden, they are unthinkable. So the wish to kill and the desire to possess are suppressed—buried—at first and later, in an effort to keep them out of consciousness, repression, an unconscious process, develops. Any thought therewith is met with abhorrance, denial and disbelief. As Freud pointed out, pride will not let us see the remotest possibility of such a thought.

However much one may wish to argue the point, a cursory observation of children from around ages four to six years or younger will provide evidence that something does take place between child and parents which is strongly suggestive of the foregoing. Consider the following observable paradigm.

    Mother to child (teasingly): My daddy.
    Child to mother (possessively): My daddy. etc.
    Father to child (teasingly): My mama. My mommie.
    Child to father (possessively): My mama or mommie. etc.

It is interesting to note that the word *mother* is very seldom, if ever used. It is also interesting to observe the intensity with which this exchange may be carried on. Not only that, but the game, if indeed it may be called a game to the child, can be further intensified if the girl resents (?) the mother's claim on the father or the boy, the father's claim on the mother. Shall we mention the resentment father or mother may feel toward the child who is getting too much attention?

I take the liberty of sharing some autobiographical data. As a lad of four, I lived in a one-room house on my grandfather's farm. One morning, my dad (daddy) came home or was home from the fields. It was fall and a fire was going in the old wood stove. Dad was sitting in a nearby chair and Mother came over and sat down on his lap. They started giggling and Dad turned to me and said, "My mommie." Mother grinned. They continued. I had been playing with a knife at the time. When he started teasing me, I got a piece of kindling, made a sharp point on it, then went over and stabbed him in the ribs on the left side. (Why didn't I use the knife?) No damage was done, but he said, "Mmm! That hurt." He frowned and rubbed the place and said, "Mustn't do that." I do not recall what happened after that. I do know I was not physically punished and I think I went outside.

Now, I shan't say more on that other than that through the years I always felt closer to my mother than I did toward my father. As a matter of fact, I always felt a strong resentment toward him. Incidentally, and I shall come back to this later, I always felt I could out best him. I recall saying to a friend of mine on the occasion of my going to college, "Well, someone in this family has to do something." My dominant fear of my father was that I would somehow, in some way, hurt him. And I must confess, I usually looked forward to his death. I felt that then I could do what I well pleased and fear of him would no longer exist: there would be no way for him to find out! But "he being dead, yet speaketh." These thoughts may seem cold but they are not intended to be. They have long been divested of their emotional charge.

Now, if you will recall, Oedipus had in fact murdered his father and married his mother. When this was brought to his attention, he was horrified. He gouged out his eyes and departed the country. He did not want to see, any more than do we, the truth involved. In anticipation, I should like to observe that both shame and guilt may be operating here with shame secondary to guilt. But it may also express the wish inherent in shame: the desire not to see is the desire not to be seen. One is reminded of the child hiding his eyes and thinking he cannot be seen. Moreover, the self-exile may imply the banishment feared in shame. But more on that later.

Moving from this episode, Freud then applied the wished-act to Hamlet,[10] observing that the wish can be just as strong in creating guilt as can the actual act. Freud argues that Hamlet did in fact desire his mother (and wish his father's death) but that he refused to see or did not wish to see these intentions. The wish to have mother (and the desire to kill father) are really the sources of his anxiety. However, they remain in the unconscious. The more they threaten instrusion into consciousness, the greater does his anxiety become. Oedipus experienced what is referred to as a conscious sense of guilt, and Hamlet, an unconscious sense of guilt. One is referred to the German doctor who rebelled at any implication of this possibility in a later writing of Freud's.[11] Dare, in honesty, we look into our own hearts?

Freud made a very fine point between the overt act as in Oedipus, and the wished-act as in Hamlet. A sense or feeling of guilt can be just as strong in the one as the other. One remembers the very strong statement of Jesus, "As a man thinketh, so is he." This raises the pregnant question, does a thought constitute a state of being? Suffice it to say that suppressing a wished-act through the mechanism of repression or refusing to admit to the wished-act can be just as disabling psychologically as suppressing the actual act, if not more so. Regarding this as it relates to melancholia, mania and compulsive disorders, I can only refer you to *General Introduction to Psychoanalysis, Group Psychology* and *The Ego and the Id.*

According to Freud, people feel a sense of guilt when they have done something they know to be bad. Then, too, people feel a sense of guilt when they become aware of the intention to do so. Adding to these, we may say that people feel a sense of guilt when they fail to comply with the expected and do the bad by omission. Or again, people feel a sense of guilt when they have done something which may be right in one place but wrong in another. Perhaps we can diagram it this way:

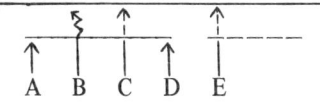

```
     ↑    ↑
  ↑  |  ↑ |
  ↑  |  ↑ |
  A  B  C  D  E
```

A = Compliance or obedience
B = Going beyond or into forbidden territory, a transgression
C = The wished-act, the intended act, the "as if" act
D = Failure to comply—omission
E = Right in one place, wrong in another (Broken line indicates lack of differentiation)

Plate 2

In Plate 2, *A* implies, I'm OK because I have obeyed. *B* implies, I am not OK because I have done the bad. *C* suggests, I am not OK because I have bad thoughts. *D* suggests, I am not OK because I have not done even the good. *E* indicates, I am not OK because what I did was all right here, but I was taught better at home.

You and I are well aware of the fact that sometimes geography determines what is right and wrong. And perhaps we each have experienced some discomfort when faced with a situation where our past conflicted with the present. Some of us could accept the old adage: "When in Rome do as the

Romans do." The rest of us remained *pure.* It is an obvious fact that the social values of one community as well as of one family or another often conflict. I suspect that is why many of us seek out a group wherever we go which pretty well agrees with our own sense of values. It spares us any adjustment in thinking as well as any feelings of discomfort (guilt and possibly shame?) which we might experience.

Now, in order for one to feel guilt, one must presuppose that a standard of behavior has been violated, especially where intent is the cause. In this case, Freud pointed out that wickedness has already been recognized as reprehensible, as something that ought not to have been executed.[12] Evil is conceived to be that which would injure or endanger the Ego. It is interesting to observe, however, that something which the Ego desires, which is normal and which gives pleasure, can also be a source of guilt. Thus, he remarks, an extraneous influence is evidently at work. Furthermore, it is this extraneous force that decides what is called good or bad. For example, one may have the love of others or he may lose the love of others. What is bad, therefore, is whatever causes one to be threatened with a loss of love. Because dread is incurred, one must desist from the act or cease to have thoughts of the act. The danger occurs when the authority finds out the fact or the intention. In either case, Freud observes, the person would behave the same way. At the early stages of development, this is called a bad conscience and the sense of guilt is only the dread of losing love. This Freud called social anxiety. And I might add, the reaction of the Ego-ideal, if accepted as a separate entity from the Super-ego, may well determine whether guilt or shame is experienced.

The mechanics of this is seen in the structure of mental processes, especially as it relates to the function of the Ego and the Superego. Guilt feelings due to the wished-act arise due to a change which occurs when the Super-ego is formed.[13] That is, through identification with and the internalization of the authority through introjection. Thus, there is an internal authority as well as an external. This adds a new dimension and two sources of guilt-feeling are now evident: the dread of the extra-psychic authority on the one hand and the intra-psychic authority (Superego) on the other. Now, if the fact or intention escapes the extra-psychic authority, it cannot escape the Superego. The extra-psychic authority compels us to renounce actual gratifying activity and the intra-psychic authority contends with the wish or desire to act. In the first, one gives up pleasure in order not to lose love. No guilt should remain unless, of course, resentment over the restriction remains. On the other hand, the wish persists and is incapable of being hidden from the Superego as is the resentment over the repulsed act. As this process continues, conscience is formed and this gives rise to further renunciation—the internal demands to live in conformity to the external standards. Conscience becomes a function of the Superego whose business it is to watch over and judge the actions and intentions of the Ego. It serves as a censor. The sense of guilt which the Ego experiences is the feeling that it is being watched. The feeling of guilt is the feeling that it has actually done or has intended to do the forbidden. Of a truth, "there is an all-seeing eye watching you."

Consider, in light of the foregoing, Adam and Eve. First a law was established by a significant person. A grave responsibility was laid upon them, perhaps beyond their capacity. However, the Infinite made allowance for any divinely-imposed limitation on his creature. A source of strength as well as an alternative course of action was provided. Man was given a choice and Adam chose what turned out to be the least preferred way of handling the conflict. He "cut" the Creator out of the act. And although He was not visibly present, Adam acted as though he had to reckon with Him. Thus, when He made his daily social call, Adam could not be found. He had hidden himself and covered this newly-discovered nakedness. In response to the Creator's call, silence. When Adam was finally discovered, there was direct and indirect displacement and only indirect incrimination. What is interesting about this whole episode is the hiding from authority because of some conceived wrong committed, the covering of nakedness, the response of silence and then the displacement, rationalization and denial.[14]

Referring back to Oedipus, you will recall we suggested that his self-mutilation (gouging out his eyes) may mean the desire not to be seen. Well, hiding one's eyes with a handkerchief, turning the head, covering the head, looking away and past the eyes of another are also ways of hiding one's self. To look into the eyes is to look into the soul. It is no less true in hiding the entire body. It is the feeling of "crawling into a hole and pulling it in after one." Nakedness may be real or psychological. People will try to cover themselves when they have exposed themselves socially—literally and figuratively. And most of us live in some dread of being exposed in public. Anyone at all familiar with psychotherapy will observe that when a person tells more than he intended in one session, the subsequent session seems to go extremely slow. Group work is no different and one should not be surprised if the person does not show up for the next session. Apologies are noticeable and acceptable cover-ups. As to whether these actions are motivated by guilt or shame will become clearer as we proceed.

In the case of Adam and Eve, it is difficult to state which they feared the most, physical pain or banishment. It is possible that they themselves did not know the full consequences of their act since the record states only that "dying, thou shalt begin to die." The record relates that both physical agony and banishment were the results of their offense, not to mention the interpersonal consequences. Perhaps this is the seriousness of *original sin:* it involves both guilt and shame. It is noteworthy that physical pain and banishment are both descriptive of the biblical concept of hell. And it seems to be an obvious observation that we are capable of creating both here and now. One does not have to have an eschatology to believe in either.

Consider the experience of David. This may appear to be a classic example of guilt but is in fact one which turns out to be a clear case of shame. David had taken Bathsheba in an act of adultery. She became pregnant. Uriah, her husband, is at the front fighting for his king and country. Well, what does a king do when he has impregnated the wife of one of his warriors? What does a man do under the circumstance if he happens to be a religious man or a man with a social conscience? Well, without too much elaboration on the matter, David tried at least six different ways to calm his conscience and all to no avail. Then Nathan, the prophet, came and ingeniously maneuvered David into self-incrimination. Horrified at his having been found out and exposed, David repented. But it was a long road. His confession contains two feelings: guilt over sin as a violation of a legal code and shame as a result of falling short of an ideal person's expectations (See Psalms 51). The first is pardoned; the latter is forgiven. He had not only broken the law of the land, he had also failed to live up to the expectations of his God and people. In passing, should one be interested, Psalms 32 is a beautiful example of a psycho-physiological autonomic visceral reaction to guilt.

Finally, with reference to St. Paul's experience, it seems obvious that he is struggling with guilt both extra-psychical and intra-psychical. As a matter of fact, this may be a very clear case to use as an illustration of a man who, up to a certain point, can live in a guilt orientated culture void of any sense of shame. This is precisely the defect in the character of the Pharisees of that time. But that is something else. In Paul's case, his legalistic orientation gave way in face of the overwhelming demands of a significant person. As indicated in Lecture III *sarks* demanded, *nomos* prohibited, and the Ego could not mediate. *Noos* agreed that the law or *nomos* was right, but the Ego in its weakness was hounded beyond its ability to function by the powerful *sunidesis.* He was indeed a miserable man. However, once he identified with the Divine *Imago,* guilt subsided and became secondary. Shame then became the thing most feared; he dreaded the occasion that might cause him to bring dishonor or reproach upon the Divine *Imago.* Years later, Paul argued that once a man realizes the real situation, he will acknowledge that he has sinned (broken the law) and is therefore guilty, and has fallen short of the glory of God and is therefore shameful (Romans 3:23).

Thus, guilt is that ill-at-ease feeling one gets when things are not right or when wrong has been committed or entertained. It is universal in extent, ethical in content and remedial in intent. Its age is that of man. Avoid it, we cannot. Evade it, we can only try. There are a thousand inroads into its sanctuary and each is guarded by a carefully selected sentry. And although well guarded, it demands release. It refuses to stay in isolation. Lady Macbeth may accent the natural beauty of her face with the latest imported Persian cosmetics in an effort to hide the secret of her heart, but she will be found wandering the halls of the palace while fast asleep symbolically washing her hands and saying, "Out, damned spot! Out!" And we may say with Shakespeare, "It takes [more than] a false face to hide what the false heart doth know."

NOTES AND BIBLIOGRAPHY

Lecture IV
1. Freud, *Lay-Analysis,* pp. 39, 41.
2. Piers and Singer, *Shame and Guilt.*
3. Freud, *Introductory Lectures.*
4. In reply to the observation that this difference is largely semantic, I would urge a closer scrutiny of the dynamics involved and the therapeutic handling of each.
5. Freud, *Introduction to Psychoanalysis,* pp. 501a-82b.
_____, *Ego and Id,* p. 703ff.
_____, *Civilization* pp. 706-7.
_____, *Lay-Analysis,* p. 43ff.
6. Mowrer, *Psychiatry and Religion,* pp. 26, 56, elsewhere.
7. On *Oedipus Rex* see:
Freud, *Origin and Development,* p. 17.
_____, *Dreams,* pp. 242-48.
_____, *Introduction to Psychoanalysis,* pp. 581-82.
_____, *Ego and Id,* p. 703ff and elsewhere.
8. Aeschylus, *Seven Against Thebes.*
9. Freud, *Origin and Development,* p. 17.
10. *Ibid.,* p. 17.
11. Freud, *Introduction to Psychoanalysis,* pp. 581-82.
12. Freud, *Civilization,* p. 706ff.
13. *Ibid.*
14. No argument over the factual authenticity or the allegorical aspects of this story is necessary. It very definitely is a prototype and history has done us a favor in preserving it for us.

"STRIPPED, NAKED I STAND" A STUDY IN SHAME

Ladies and gentlemen, greater than the guilt he cannot feel is the shame he is made to experience, so *Branded* becomes the scorn of all guilt-ridden people who scapegoat (displace) their own sense of shame upon a person who has supposedly failed in the service of his country. Stripped of all rank and privileges, *Branded* stands naked before his contemporaries and the world of viewers. He is scorned, rejected and becomes a reproach wherever he goes. And wherever he goes, he is made to suffer—rightly or wrongly, we do not know. But privately, I suspect we think wrongly, because secretly we recoil at the sight of his humiliation, perhaps vicariously, because of our own fear of exposure and humiliation. Such is the power of identification.

I cannot accent too strongly the words *stripped, exposure* and *humiliation*. One has only to imagine his own feeling of horror at being stood before people and literally stripped naked. Even if he had committed a crime for which he might be adjudged guilty and for the same have a sense of guilt, the hurt would only be compounded by shame.

Shame is greater than guilt because it antedates guilt. The child is made to experience shame long before he knows guilt. The feeling bad (or bad conscience to which Freud refers) comes earlier than four or six years. It comes from the earliest impressions made at various times from the nipple to the "potty." Such expressions as "You little stinker," "You dirty little boy" or "Shame upon you" are shaming remarks. Or, he observes the crook, back and forth movement of the forefinger with the "tha, tha, tha" sound made with the tongue against the upper palate accented by a slight sucking sound. Or again, he sees the crossing and movement of the forefingers on each hand. Or, he feels the hurt look and the turning of the back of a loved one and perhaps the long silence with the look of hurt. These are greater punishment than a stern look, the pointed finger and/or the switch. Nothing stings worse than rejection, nonacceptance and being forsaken. And I suspect, these early impressions are fortified by the fear of a parent who says, "What will the neighbors think?" or, "Don't disgrace, dishonor or bring reproach upon the family name!"

Where there is no guilt, there is no sense of right or wrong; but where there is no shame, there is no social awareness. Guilt is rectified by rationalization and pardon. It is punished by inflicting or fear of having inflicted physical harm. Shame is rectified by face-saving actions and forgiveness. It is punished by being forsaken or banished. A little nine-year-old stated the difference so succinctly when she said, "Guilt is the shame you can talk about, shame is the guilt you cannot talk about."

But all this is anticipating. The main reason shame has been neglected lies in the acceptance of a theory of personality based upon an ethic that is basically legalistic. I refer of course to Freud and the law ethic of the Jewish community and any other system which holds to a legal code of ethics. This goes for theology also, Protestantism not excepted.

Theologically speaking, this may be a good place to start in making a distinction between shame and guilt. The law is impersonal. It knows no mercy; only a person can be merciful. Guilt is related to an ethical system; shame is related to a person. Guilt is incurred when a person violates a code of conduct in fact or in fancy. Shame is felt when a person lets another person or a group of people down. Guilt can be pardoned; shame, forgiven. Shame faces a significant person and the image of self as it now is before the person or persons whom one has failed.

Be that as it may, we are interested in the mechanism of

shame as it may or may not relate either to a theory of personality or a theology of persons. Now, if one can accept the Superego and the Ego-ideal as separate entities (to use Freud's terminology), then we may postulate the difference accordingly. Guilt arises from conflict between the Ego and the Superego; shame, from a conflict between the Ego and the Ego-ideal. At this point, one should begin to see that the distinction is more than semantic. The dynamic is entirely different even though one may easily dissolve into the other. However, where the two are working together, they will usually produce what both the psychologist and the theologian should more aptly refer to as *metanoia* or repentance. But, again, this is anticipating.

Let us return to our primary instructor. As mentioned in the foregoing lecture, Freud did not deal with shame, per se, as a feeling experienced by the Ego. However, the question was raised regarding the possibility of his notion of inferiority[1] being developed into a feeling of shame. Since at least one of his students has entertained this idea, we may not be reading too much back into Freud under the circumstances.

If you will recall, Freud stated in 1932[2] that the feeling of inferiority was, like guilt, the expression of tension between the Ego and the Superego. However, he continued that "The sense of inferiority and the sense of guilt are exceedingly difficult to distinguish." Other analytic writers, Symonds[3] for example (and although not an analyst, but a psychiatrist who is widely read in the area of religion, Tournier[4]), speaks of guilt and inferiority as if they were together, yet with distinction. Lynd[5] makes a strong case for inferiority to mean shame. However, the most clear-cut distinction yet to be found is that of Piers and Singer.[6] Attention is also called to *The Three Christs of Ypsilanti*[7] and a very fine article in the *Psychiatric Spectator* by Wurmser.[8] It seems only fair to say that I had made this distinction long before I had read any of these works, but due to my inexperience, I was not able to develop it psychologically.

Piers[9] makes the following observations. First, guilt arises out of the conflict between the Ego and the Superego whenever a boundary set up by the Superego is touched or transgressed. (He does not refer to intention.) Shame, on the other hand, arises out of the conflict between the Ego and the Ego-ideal when a goal presented by the Ego-ideal is not being reached. It indicates a real short-coming. Guilt anxiety accompanies transgression and thus the fear of punishment. In its most primeval form it is physical harm (mutilation or castration). Shame accompanies failure and thus the fear of abandonment. In its most primeval form it is banishment. Parenthetically, I have observed that most Marines I have worked with would prefer a physical beating to a mark on the record. The record is an extension of their ego. It is conceived to be the Marine himself. And I suspect that most of us would prefer a beating to the hurt look, the long silence, the turning and walking away and/or the banishment to a room. The irrational threat implied in shame anxiety is banishment and not mutilation (or castration) as in guilt. Or, as Scripture indicates, "If thine eye [hand or foot] offend thee, pluck it out [cut it off] and cast it from thee' (Matthew 18:7-9). Or, "Depart from me . . . for I never knew you" (Matthew 25:41-46). Apparently, it is better to enter into a state of bliss, maimed, than it is to be banished intact to hell. Degrees of punishment have always been a theological maxim.

Second, the Ego-ideal appears to contain a core of narcissistic omnipotence. Self-love is greater than object love! If this is true, it may account for "rebellion through obedience." That is, "This is what you always said I would do—that I could not succeed—so I act in accordance with your contempt and lack of confidence (in me), well knowing that I am hurting your pride and ambition (for me)." Thus, the ultimate in retaliation may be suicide. As Menninger said, "There is homicide in every suicide."[10] And as Berne suggests,[11] one has to decide who is trying to kill whom: the parent, the child or the child, the parents?

Third, the Ego-ideal represents the sum of the positive identification of the Ego with the parental image or the significant persons or persons in the individual's life. This may explain the action of a chief petty officer I had as a patient in one of my groups during my third year of training. He had very little trouble with rules and regulations. However, one dominant theme was the respect he had for his father. He wanted to be as good a man as his "old man." In his own way, the chief got around many of the rules (no infraction was ever enough to get him into trouble and then he would joke and rationalize those). But any fear of failure as a son sent his blood pressure sky high. In this case, I would suspect the negative traits of the father had become positive traits for the son.

Fourth, the Ego-ideal contains later identifications of social role when the siblings and peers are more significant in influencing behavior. Freud had this in mind when he talked about social anxiety. What happens here is related to the shifting of authority from parental influence to siblings, to little Charlie Brown next door, to groups, teachers, coaches, etc. Finally, the Ego-ideal is in continuous awareness of the Ego's potentialities. Thus, early parental expectations and present personal desires may become a source of shame and guilt if there is conflict. For example, "My old man always wanted me to be... but I am interested in doing this or that." This may account for failure in some people: not having permission to succeed, they can only fail. (See Plate 3)

Now, if shame is the tension felt between the Ego and the Ego-ideal, then shame occurs whenever goals and/or images (ideal or significant persons) presented by the Ego-ideal are not reached.

> Goal ⟶ failure ⟶ fear of contempt ⟶ shame ⟶ fear of abandonment (death by emotional starvation) ⟶ and deeper yet, separation anxiety. (Hell, then, becomes a reality in time.)

The following diagram may be of help:

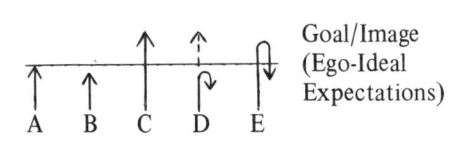

```
        ↑  ↑   ↻      Goal/Image
    ↑   ↑   │  ↻   │  (Ego-Ideal
    ↑   ↑   │  ↻   │   Expectations)
    A   B   C  D   E
```

A = Measuring up to what the Ego-ideal expects
B = Not measuring up: falling short, failure
C - Going beyond the expected, "beating the father," triumph, succeeding
D = Not having permission to succeed, "One cannot do better than the father."
E = May succeed but not be able to stand success. This may tie in with guilt. Success may mean dishonoring the father (Success-failure syndrome).

Plate 3

I should like now to diagram guilt and shame as they might appear in the structural mode between the Superego and Ego-ideal.

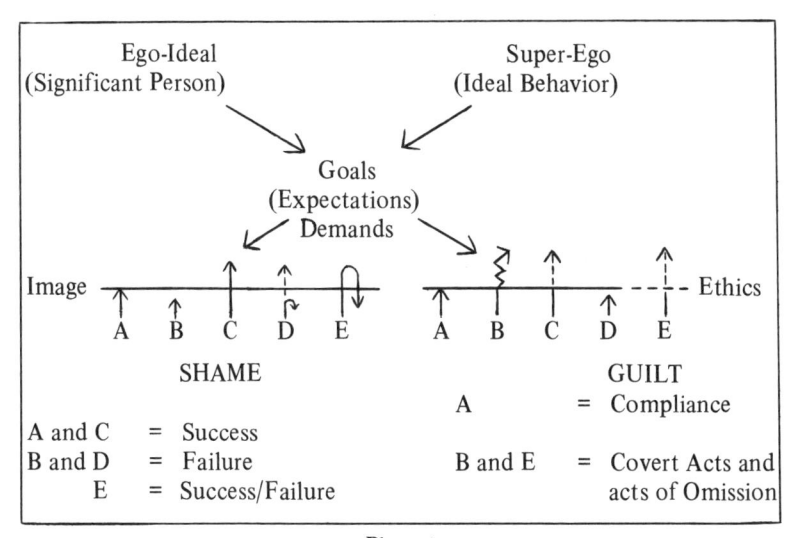

```
    Ego-Ideal                    Super-Ego
(Significant Person)          (Ideal Behavior)
           ↘                   ↙
               Goals
           (Expectations)
           ↙  Demands  ↘
Image  ─┬─┬─┬──┬──┬──  ─┬─┬─┬──┬──┬─ ─ ─ Ethics
        A B C  D  E     A B C  D  E
              SHAME              GUILT
                              A      = Compliance
A and C  = Success
B and D  = Failure            B and E = Covert Acts and
      E  = Success/Failure              acts of Omission
```

Plate 4

I should now like to refer to the paper of Wurmser[1,2] in which he pointed out the difference between shame and guilt and their relation to depersonalization and depression. He postulated that it is the denial of shame anxiety which underlies almost uniformly the severe chronic forms of depersonalization. He suggested there is probably a similar correlation between depersonalization and the unconscious feelings of shame as there is between depression and unconscious feelings of guilt. The wish in the feeling of shame is, "I want to disappear as the person I have shown myself to be. I want to be different than I am." (See Erik Ericson, *Childhood and Society*.[13]) What the patient indicates, according to Wurmser, is "I am not this (person); this is someone else, not me."

He observed that the dominant fear in shame and guilt may help to make a further distinction between the two. In shame, it is fears of exposure, scorn, failure, abandonment and self-contempt. In guilt, it is fears of attack, condemnation and retaliation, mutilation and self-hatred. He further observed that in the shame psychosis the main dangers are suicide and starving with the goal: the desire not to be seen anymore. He also stated that people suffering from a sense of shame do not respond too well to somatic treatment but improve markedly under long, intensive, analytically orientated psychotherapy.

The following case may have some bearing upon these observations. While at the clinic, another chief petty officer was brought in for treatment. He was quickly diagnosed as experiencing a depressive reaction. Electro-shock therapy was prescribed as the treatment of choice. And, it worked wonders. He bounded back with energy, squared away and requested more. When this attitude persisted, he was presented to the staff. He looked depressed. He acted depressed. He gave a confused story of his experiences in Vietnam. Having just come from that area, I was able to offer a correct interpretation of the situation as far as geography and enemy position were concerned. I pointed this out to the staff and the question was raised as to whether he was confabulating. Well, during the course of the interview, one could observe in him a little boy pleading with all these omnipotent and omniscient people for acceptance and forgiveness: "Please don't put me out of the Navy." Over and over he made the request. His voice was soft. His eyes swelled with tears. In both his eyes and his voice one could see the intensity of his plea. His chin quivered and I could not help but recall an old country ballad heard often as a child: "Don't make me go to bed and I'll be good." With the chief, any form of punishment but banishment (discharge) was acceptable. But you do not treat shame and guilt the same way! Well, one other doctor and myself argued for a shame anxiety reaction as opposed to guilt but to no avail. Shame anxiety was unknown!

I now refer to *The Three Christs of Ypsilanti.*[14] This is the story of three deluded men, each of whom claimed to be Christ, and their experiences of living together in a large state hospital. Rokeach was interested in one particular question: What would happen if suddenly one Christ were confronted with the others? I shan't go into detail about this experiment. I can only urge that you read it. From a theological point of view, it may be a new beginning for a fresh look at the psychology of belief. Suffice it to say, the author concludes that in Clyde and Joseph, the dominant theme of sexual confusion seemed to be tinged with a sense of shame over feelings stemming from incompetence as a male. These are not guilt-ridden Christs, they are more preoccupied with being great than with being good. Clyde is Christ because he needs to be "the biggest one." Joseph is God, Christ and the Holy Ghost because these are the biggest personages one can be. If there were a super-God, Joseph would have been super-God. For these men, Christ is the epitome of greatness.

Leon, on the other hand, is dominated by guilt because of his forbidden sexual and aggressive impulses. He is forever tormented with inadmissible longings for persons of both sexes, with his need to prove to himself that he is a potent male, with an awareness of wrong-doing about his masturbatory efforts to test and prove his potency, and with feelings of projected hostility toward others. Leon wants to be good which means not to have bad thoughts and do bad things. To him, the epitome of goodness is Christ.

I wish I could go further with this in St. Paul, but it cannot be related to his experience in Romans 7:14-25. However, the notion of shame does become his dominant fear as a Christian. Falling short of the glory of God (the Divine *Imago*) is the greatest threat he can possibly imagine to his existence. For him, Christ must be glorified in himself at all costs. He could not relish the possibility of standing before God, stripped, exposed to Divine scrutiny and be found wanting in his likeness to Christ. He must be "clothed" with the Spirit and have on "the robe of righteousness." And I might add, his prayer for his young son in the faith was, "Timothy, don't be ashamed of Christ nor of me, his prisoner."

In closing, what shall I say about Peter and Judas? I can only suggest that you pursue these in your private study. In addition, it seems that Jesus based his whole teaching on the importance of shame: "The Son always pleases the Father." And it seems that both Jesus and Paul have gone beyond Freud in dealing with the mainsprings of human behavior. But thanks to him, we do understand our own faith a little better.

NOTES AND BIBLIOGRAPHY

Lecture V
1. Freud, *Ego and Id*, pp. 706, 713c; *Introductory Lectures*, p. 852; *Lay-Analysis*, pp. 39, 41.
2. Freud, *Introductory Lectures*, p. 852.
3. M. Symonds, *Dynamics*.
4. Tournier, *Guilt and Grace*.
5. Lynd, *Shame*, p. 22.
6. Piers and Singer, *Shame and Guilt*.
7. Rokeach, *Three Christs*.
8. Wurmser, "Depersonalization and Shame."
9. Piers and Singer, *Shame and Guilt*.
10. Menninger, *Man Against Himself*, p. 32.
11. Berne, *Transactional Analysis*.

This statement, per se, is not found in this book. However, a knowledge of Berne's basic assumptions will help one to understand the statement which was made at one of the weekly scientific meetings of the San Francisco Transactional Analysis Association of which the writer is a member (1966).

A young lad in one of my therapy groups stated that he felt the only way he could get rid of the voice he was always hearing was to kill himself. He identified the voice as that of his father and described it as being in his head (motioning with his hand).

12. Wurmser, *Depersonalization*.
13. Erickson, *Childhood and Society*, p. 252.
14. Rokeach, *Three Christs*, p. 336f.

On the day this was written, I interviewed a young man who professed quite blatantly that he was a homosexual. I raised the question as to whether he felt bad about a behavior which society, by and large, frowned upon. He replied, "Only when caught." I asked, how do you feel then? He answered, "Like hiding my face." I then asked which meant the most to him, to be good or to be great? He replied, "Oh, to be great. Man, I mean to be the greatest. I want to be so big, they'll have to look up to me." He then volunteered the information that he had been quite fat as a youth but was now trim, beautiful and good looking. "Man, I'm good looking. But now I'm trim and they want me. I mean I'm going to be the greatest." I intervened, "That sounds like Napoleon." It was a mistake.

In regards to the Christs of Ypsilanti, one recalls the grace learned by many children:

> God is Great,
> God is Good,
> Let us thank Him for our food.

Both the greatness and the goodness of God are attributes with which the "three lost men" of Ypsilanti struggle. No one combined the two in himself. They are only half-gods!

End

BIBLIOGRAPHY
I. BOOKS

Aeschylus, *The Seven Against Thebes* (Chicago: Encyclopaedia Britannica, Inc., 1952). Great Books series.

American Hand Book of Psychiatry (New York: Basic Books, Inc., Publishers, 1959). Edited by Silvano Ariete.

Arieti, Silvano, *The Intra-Psychic Self* (New York: Basic Books, Inc., Publishers, 1957).

Arendt, W. F. and Gingrich, F. W., *A Greek-English Lexicon of the New Testament* (Chicago: The University of Chicago Press, 1956).

Barth, Karl, *Shorter Commentary on Romans,* (Richmond, John Knox Press, 1959).

Berne, Eric, *Transactional Analysis in Psychotherapy* (New York: Grove Press, Inc., 1960).

Brunner, Emil, *The Letter of Paul to the Romans* (Philadelphia: The Westminster Press, 1959).

Denny, James, "St. Paul's Epistle to the Romans" in *The Expositor's Greek Testament,* Edited by W. Robertson Nicoll (Grand Rapids: Wm. B. Eerdmans Publishing Co., n.d.).

Erickson, Erik, *Childhood and Society* (New York: W. W. Norton and Company, Inc., 1950).

Ford, Donald H. and Urban, Hugh B., *Systems of Psychotherapy* (New York: John Wiley and Sons, Inc., 1963).

Freud, Sigmund, *Great Books series* (Chicago: Encyclopaedia Britannica, Inc., 1952).
The Origin and Development of Psycho-Analysis (1910).
The Interpretation of Dreams (1900).
On Narcissim (1914).
Instincts and Their Vicissitudes (1915).
A General Introduction to Psycho-Analysis (1915-17).
Beyond the Pleasure Principle (1920).
Group Psychology and the Analysis of the Ego (1921).
The Ego and The Id (1923).
Civilization and Its Discontents (1929).

New Introductory Lectures on Psycho-Analysis (1932).

———, *Collected Papers* (New York: Basic Books, Inc., 1959). 5 Vols.

———, *Moses and Monotheism* (New York: Vintage Book, 1955).

———, *The Future of an Illusion* (Garden City: Doubleday Anchor Book, 1957).

———, *The Question of Lay Analysis* (Garden City: Doubleday Anchor Books, 1964).

Godet, F. L., *Commentary to the Epistle to the Romans* (Grand Rapids: Zondervan Publishing House, 1956).

Hall, Calvin and Lindsey, Gordner, *Theories of Personality* (New York: John Wiley and Sons, Inc., 1957).

Healy, William, Bonner, Audusta F., Bowers, Anne Lee, *The Structure and Meaning of Psychoanalysis* (New York: Alfred A. Knopf, 1930).

Lampl-de Groote, Jeanne, *The Development of the Mind* (New York: International Universities Press Inc., 1965).

Lenski, R. C. H., *The Interpretation of St. Paul's Epistle to the Romans* (Columbus: Wartburg Press, 1945).

Lynd, Helen Merrel, *On Shame and the Search for Identity* (New York: Science Editors, Inc., 1961).

Moffatt, James, *The Bible: A New Translation* (New York: Harper and Brothers Publishers, 1922).

Mowrer, O. Hobart, *Learning Theory and Behavior* (New York: John Wiley and Sons, Inc., 1960).

———, *The Crisis In Psychiatry and Religion* (New York: Van Nostrand Company, Inc., 1961).

———, *The New Group Therapy* (New York: Van Nostrand Company, Inc., 1964).

Nunberg, Herman, *Practice and Theory of Psychoanalysis* (New York: International Universities Press, 1965), Vol. I.

———, *Principles of Psychoanalysis* (New York: International Universities Press, 1955).

Piers, Gerhart and Singer, Milton, *Shame and Guilt (A Psychoanalytic and Cultural Study),* (Springfield: Charles C. Thomas, Publ, 1953).

Plato, "Phaedo," *The Dialogues of Plato* (New York: Random House, 1937). Vol. I.

Rapport, David, *Collected Papers* (New York: Basic Books, Inc., 1967).

Reik, Theodor, *Of Love and Lust* (New York: The Noonday Press, 1941).

Robert, Marthe, *The Psychoanalytic Revolution* (New York: Harcourt, Brace and World, Inc., 1966).
Rokeach, Milton, *The Three Christs of Ypsilanti* (New York: Alfred A. Knoph, 1964).
Symonds, Percival M., *The Dynamics of Human Adjustment* (New York: Appleton-Century-Crofts, Inc., 1946).
Thayer, Joseph Henry, *A Greek-English Lexicon of the New Testament* (New York: American Book Company, 1889).
Tournier, Paul, *Guilt and Grace* (New York: Harper and Row, Publishers, 1962).
White, Ernest, *The Christian Life and the Unconscious* (New York: Harper and Brothers, 1955).

II. PERIODICALS

Blain, Daniel, "Organized Religion and Mental Health." *Journal of Religion and Health,* January, 1965, Vol. 4, No. 2.
Bruder, Ernest E., "The Minister and Mental Health."*Pastoral Psychology,* May, 1960, Vol. 11, No. 104.
Folles, Stanley F., "Role of Religion in the Mental Health Program." *Journal of Religion and Health,* July, 1965, Vol. 4, No. 4.
Leslie, Robert C., "Cooperation Between Psychotherapist and Pastoral Counselors in the United States." *Pastoral Psychology,* November, 1961, Vol. 12, No. 118.
Reissner, Albert, "Religion and Classical Psychotherapy." *Christian Century,* April, 1961.
Steinzor, Bernard, "The Minister as a Social Therapist." *Journal of Religion and Health,* October, 1965, Vol. 4, No. 5.
Wurmser, Leon, "Depersonalization and Shame." *Psychiatric Spectator* (Sandoz Pharmaceuticals, Vol. II, No. 9).

MAY 24 1973

APR 21 1978

JUN 30 1978

JUN 1 1979

JUN 1 1981

JAN 31 1984

JUN 30 1987

FEB 8 1973